One very wet and w̵.
I was looking at the garden out of my kitchen window. The rain was teeming down and the Silver Birch tree was taking a real battering from the gales.

As I looked, I noticed on the bottom branch, right against the trunk of the tree, a little dove sitting calmly and peacefully, waiting out the storm. It was totally undisturbed by it's uncomfortable, noisy and chaotic surroundings.

A lovely truth came to my mind. It is possible to have complete peace and calm in our hearts, even in the middle of the turmoil and storms of life.

That little dove had settled on the strongest part of the branch - next to the trunk, and was perfectly safe.

God has promised that He will keep us in perfect peace if our hearts and minds are trusting in Him.

Isaiah Chapter 26 verse 3

"You will keep in perfect peace him whose mind is steadfast, because he trusts in you."

Faith

According to the Dictionary 'Faith' is 'complete trust or confidence', but faith has to be in something.

If asked, what would you say your faith was in? Would it be in your own abilities; your family; your wealth perhaps? Any one of those could let you down.

My answer would be "in God". Why? Because I know He can be trusted. I have tried and proved that His Word is true. In many areas of life, my faith has been put to the test and I've always found God is faithful.

Does your faith, in whatever you have chosen to place it, have a firm foundation? Do you have complete confidence in life, no matter what happens, that all will be well? You can, if your faith is in a secure place - the only truly secure place is in God, He will never let you down.

Romans 10 verse 11

"As the scripture says, "Anyone who trusts In Him will never be put to shame."

The shepherd and his sheep

Spring is such a lovely time of year. The cold dark days of winter are gone and everything is bursting with new life. It's lovely to watch the sheep with their little newborn lambs.

One day whilst driving through the countryside, I noticed a flock of sheep and lambs in a field, all gathered around a farmer, looking up at him in trust and anticipation of being fed or led to new pasture.

Sheep are often considered dumb creatures because they follow each other and are prone to wander and get into trouble. We can be a bit like that too. We follow the crowd and current trends and get into difficulty because we don't see the dangers of living apart from God.

In the Bible we are likened to sheep that need a shepherd. A real shepherd knows his sheep, understands their ways and they respond to him. He cares for their lives and won't let them perish. He doesn't drive them, He leads and they follow. Isn't that just like Jesus with us!

John 10 verse 27

"My sheep listen to my voice; I know them and they follow me. I give them eternal life, and they shall never perish; no one can snatch them out of my hand."

Family

I come from a family of five children; it may be you were an only child, but like every family on earth we have our 'ups' and 'downs'! A lot of families get on well together, but sometimes over something quite trivial they can be torn apart and it can be like all out war!

Although we may share the same parents and all be similar in character and appearance, we are still complete individuals, each with different ideas and temperaments.

Most of us will have heard the saying 'You can pick your friends, but you can't choose your family'. True as that may be, it's not a good way to think.

However close or otherwise we may be as a family perhaps we should bear in mind that it was God who put us together, and we should love, support and care for each other as much as we can. Remember - God doesn't make mistakes!

Romans 12 verse 18

"If it is possible, as far as it depends on you, live at peace with everyone."

How's your Heart?

A lot of attention these days is directed towards our physical wellbeing, in particular the condition of our hearts.

We have exercise routines for our cardiovascular health; we have special foods to reduce our cholesterol; and are told to avoid too much fat in our diets. Of course it is important to maintain a healthy heart.

It isn't just our physical heart that needs looking after. The very centre or 'heart' of us is our soul, and that too requires attention.

Have we become 'hard-hearted' towards the needs of others and the things of God? It can easily happen as everything today is geared up to our becoming self-indulgent, self-centred and looking after 'No. 1'.

Perhaps it would be good now and then to have a little spiritual health check to make sure our 'hearts' are first of all right with God and also 'tender' towards others.

Psalm 139 verses 23-24

"Search me, O God, and know my heart; test me and know my anxious thoughts. See if there is any offensive way in me, and lead me in the way everlasting."

Forgiveness

On many occasions when I have been watching the news on TV, I have heard a bereaved parent, friend or relative announcing that they will "never forgive" the person who committed the dreadful act against their loved one.

Perhaps we don't realise the gravity of such a statement. As hard or even impossible as it may seem, we must forgive. If not there are consequences for us, which will be far worse than the 'wrong' we feel we have suffered. That consequence is, that unless we forgive others, we ourselves will not be forgiven by God!

In the Lord's Prayer we say "Forgive us our sins, as we forgive those who sin against us". We all need forgiveness, that's why Jesus died - so that we can be forgiven. If we ask forgiveness from God and forgive others; then one day when we stand before Him - as we all will - our 'slate' will be clean and we will be accepted by Him. Have you got some unforgiven issues? It's worth getting them sorted out. You'll feel so much better!

Colossians 3 verse 13

"Bear with each other and forgive whatever grievances you may have against one another. Forgive as the Lord forgave you."

For such a time as this!

At some point in our lives, I'm sure that certain questions come into our minds, one being, why we were born where and when we were and not at another time or place in history?

Many of us have 'looked over the fence' and wondered what it would be like to have someone else's life. Recent TV shows have given people the chance to swap lives with someone else, but most of them were glad to get back to the way they were!

We may wonder what our lives are all about sometimes, but God has made us who we are, with a plan and purpose for our lives and we are here "for such a time as this"!

One beautiful young girl named Esther who lived in Bible times, went from being an orphan to becoming a Queen. God had planned that because of her position as Queen she would save her people from being killed. She had been born for that particular purpose and moment in time.

Psalm 33 verse 11

"But the plans of the Lord stand firm forever, the purposes of His heart through all generations."

My Footprint

These days we hear a lot about our 'carbon footprint' - but what is it?

It's the measure of impact our activities have on the environment as we go about our daily lives. It includes things like driving our cars and our use of energy - gas, electricity, oil etc. because all this affects the world around us.

It's not a bad thing to be reminded of the impact we have on our natural world, but we also need to consider the spiritual impact we have too.

So how can we leave a positive 'spiritual footprint'? By centering our lives around God, and allowing Him to help us make a difference to the lives of other people by our attitudes and behaviour.

It's important that folks remember us for the kind of people we are and not just what we do.

Psalm 33 verses 13-15

"From heaven the Lord looks down and sees all mankind; From His dwelling place He watches all who live on earth He who forms the hearts of all, who considers everything they do."

Friends

Friends are very important in life. We all need a special person we can trust and share things with; someone who will be there for us in good and bad times; someone we can rely on.

However close our friendships are, there are times when things can go wrong. A thoughtless word or action can cause a breakdown in a friendship and things are not the same until we apologise and forgive.

Friendship is a two-way thing. To have a friend, you need to be a friend!

There is one friend who will never hurt or let us down; who always has our best interests at heart, but sadly we often only turn to Him in a crisis. That seems so unfair, when He loves us so much and is always there for us.

If your friendship with the Lord has lapsed or perhaps has never really existed, then why not make it a two-way friendship today?

Proverbs 18 verse 24

"A man of many companions may come to ruin, but there is a friend who sticks closer than a brother."

The best is yet to come!

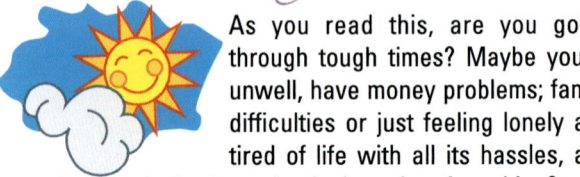

As you read this, are you going through tough times? Maybe you're unwell, have money problems; family difficulties or just feeling lonely and tired of life with all its hassles, and you're wondering just what is the point of anything?

Well, it could be you need reminding that you are precious; you are unique and you are on this earth right now because God planned it that way and has a purpose for your life!

Most of the great characters in history, including those in the Bible experienced bad times and many difficulties, but that's partly what made them great - they persevered and overcame them. We can too, with God's help. So put your trust in Him.

Why not have a little talk with God, He's always listening, and although it may not seem like it right now - "the best is yet to come" according to the Bible.

Jeremiah 29 verse 11

*"For I know the plans I have for you", declares the Lord
"Plans to prosper you and not to harm you, plans to give
you hope and a future."*

Wisdom

I've often wondered why it is that an owl is used to symbolise wisdom?

One theory is that it's because of its nocturnal vigilance. It will sit, watch, wait and listen, and is associated with the diligence of a studious scholar or wise elder!

One thing clearly missing in our society today is wisdom! Wisdom according to the Dictionary is 'soundness of judgement; knowledge and understanding'. But how do we get wisdom?

True wisdom comes from God. King Solomon was a very wise man because he revered God and asked for wisdom. Wisdom is available to us all - we simply have to ask!

We have a lot of knowledge these days, but because God has been pushed out of our society, we lack wisdom. We can start by making sure we ourselves are right with God because 'the fear of the Lord is the beginning of wisdom".

Proverbs 2 verse 6

"For the Lord gives wisdom, and from His mouth come knowledge and understanding."

The Tulip

During recent years there has been a huge emphasis on home design and accessorizing, and tulips have become very popular as a decoration either in silk or fresh flowers.

I often have a vase of fresh tulips in my home. They are serene, elegant flowers, but do need lots of water. If I forget to top them up every day, they flop over the edge of the vase with their heads pointing down until I give them a drink!

They remind me that we can sometimes feel low, and walk with our heads bowed carrying the weight of our worries and anxieties, until someone encourages us.

Many years ago I came across a little poem, I have no idea who wrote it, but it stayed with me and went something like this: "Look at me" says the tulip, "when you are feeling low, discouraged and disgruntled and life has lost its glow". "Look at me" says the tulip "and lift toward heaven your cup, And let the sunshine of God's love, come and fill you up!"

Psalm 42 verse 5

"Why are you downcast, O my soul? Why so disturbed within me? Put your hope in God…"

Do you have a 'yes' face?

We always say that first impressions count. When you are walking along the road or through the shopping Mall and folks look at you, what do they see - how is your countenance?

Would they feel they could approach you if they needed help? Would they see a relaxed look, an easy smile, and detect a friendly attitude. Or do we look unapproachable, as if we're on a mission with no time to stop, and we're carrying the weight of the world on our shoulders?

The way others perceive us matters a great deal. The Bible says "a happy heart makes the face cheerful." If your heart is at peace, it will reflect in your face. That in turn will affect those you meet in the street.

So smile at folks today and see the difference it makes!

Proverbs 15 verse 30

"A cheerful look brings joy to the heart…"

Giving

In recent years I have been involved in caring for elderly relatives, several of whom were in a care home. Whilst making regular visits to them I learned a very important lesson. No amount of gifts, flowers, cards etc. that they received, although much appreciated, could take the place of a personal visit.

When someone is in hospital, housebound or living alone, the nicest thing we can do, and something which does so much good, is to give our time and visit them.

A smiling face, a word of comfort a hug and a prayer, can make the world of difference - it's the personal touch. Real Christian giving is the giving of ourselves. We can give money and things at any time, but sacrificial giving is using our precious time for the good of others and in God's service.

Proverbs 11 verse 25

"A generous man will prosper; he who refreshes others will himself be refreshed."

A good recipe

One of my hobbies is making Wedding Cakes. Whilst thinking about what goes into a celebration cake, I compared the ingredients with what it takes to make up a Church!

Fruits: represent the variety of personalities and gifts. *Sugar, Butter, Eggs:* the common interests that bind us together. *Flour:* gives texture and support - like our friends and Minister who encourage us. *Spices:* add flavour - like those who bring new ideas and ministries. *Salt:* enhances the flavour - like our faith as we share it with others. *Milk:* keeps the cake moist and fresh - like the Word of God applied to our lives.

The cake is baked to consolidate the mixture. The 'heat' of difficult times draws us closer together as a fellowship. Marzipan covers the cake - like the building where we all meet under one roof with the same purpose - to worship. The white icing - representing the beauty and purity of God, who is over us all and covers us with His love.

Romans 12 verse 5

"So in Christ we who are many form one body, and each member belongs to all the others."

Communication

Love them or hate them, mobile phones are here to stay! In many ways they are a nuisance and intrusive, but in other ways they have got people talking and keeping in touch more. The same applies to other electronic means of communication. We have e-mail, and different social networking sites.

Communication is important and keeps people from being isolated, but have we gone too much the other way and no longer give time to personal contact?

Huge amounts of time these days are spent on the Internet, on mobile phones and watching TV - another information source. But how much time have we left to communicate with the one who matters most - the Lord!

If we compare the time we spend in prayer with the time we spend on other means of communication, we would probably feel very ashamed. Yet we wonder why things don't go well for us. Could it be we have our 'wires crossed'!

Ephesians 6 verse 18

"And pray in the Spirit on all occasions with all kinds of prayers and requests. With this in mind, be alert and always keep on praying for all the saints."

A lesson from the Oyster!

Have you ever had a stone in your shoe, something stuck in your tooth, or a bit of dust in your eye? Any of those will really irritate and you don't get any relief until it's removed!

There will always be things and people who come into our lives that frustrate and irritate us, but how do we deal with them?

A lovely example of turning irritations into something positive is the little oyster. When it gets a bit of sand or grit inside its shell, it secretes a substance known as nacre, and over a period of time wraps the irritant in layer upon layer. Eventually the irritant disappears and a beautiful pearl is formed by the nacre surrounding it.

When things irritate you, do you lose your temper, or will you allow God to help you turn them into 'pearls' of patience, kindness and perseverance that will encourage others, because you have learned to deal with them bit by bit so they are no longer a problem.

Proverbs 10 verse 12

"…Love covers over all wrongs."

Forget-me-not!

How's your memory? As we get older, the thing that seems to affect most of us is forgetfulness!

Because I keep forgetting things, or forget what I was doing because I've been distracted, my husband brought me a little hand-held computer with a 'brain-training' programme! Apparently it helps to keep your memory sharp. The only down side is that I keep forgetting where I've put it!!

I've often heard folks say "I'll never forget what that person did for me, they were so kind." We will readily remember a good deed someone does, yet why is it that we so easily forget that Jesus gave His life for us?

We often take for granted all the things He gives us every day. Perhaps we should train ourselves to read the Bible and talk to God in prayer regularly. That way we will remember Him! In my garden I have a little flower called 'Forget-me-not' - is that what God is saying to us today?

Deuteronomy 6 verse 12

"Be careful that you do not forget the Lord."

Observe the Cat!

Have you ever watched a cat when it's resting? It is totally relaxed. It will stretch, preen, purr and roll from side to side, but is completely content. I've  often watched my cat and thought 'What a life'!

One of the current 'buzzwords' is 'chill out'. If you ask someone what they have done over the weekend, their answer very often will be "I just chilled out"! It's a strange use of the word really as 'chill' means 'an unpleasant feeling of coldness' or to be 'frightened or horrified'! But these days, its use usually means to 'relax'.

It's not always easy to relax and rest when things are troubling us, or we are in difficult situations. However, if we are really trusting God and living Godly lives, we will be able to rest and be content in Him.

I have a 'sticker' in my kitchen which says "Relax, God is in control". What more do we need?!

Proverbs 19 verse 23

"The fear of the Lord leads to life: then one rests content, untouched by trouble."

Be Prepared!

Just recently, the Environment Agency contacted the residents in the Coastal Area in which we live, advising us that there was a strong possibility of flooding to our homes from the excessively high Spring Tides.

This caused a mixed reaction! Some said "It won't happen to us"; others were very concerned and made the recommended preparations. Thankfully the tide didn't cause flooding, but at least some of us were prepared.

Throughout our lives we make preparations for future events and put a lot of effort into being ready - it may be a wedding, a birthday, a holiday, a house move, to mention just a few.

But have we made preparations for Eternity? This life isn't all there is. We are told quite clearly in the Bible that we need to be ready to meet God one day, and since we don't know exactly when that day will be, surely it would be sensible to be prepared!

Matthew 24 verse 42

"Therefore keep watch, because you do not know on what day your Lord will come"

The Frozen Rose

One freezing January morning as I looked out of the window at the garden, I thought how sad and bare everything seemed. Then something caught my eye.

There in the flower border, all on its own standing tall and proud, was a beautiful yellow rose in full bloom. I could hardly believe it, so I went out for a closer look.

That single rose had come from a plant I had given up for dead. The Rose was frozen solid. It looked beautiful but its sweet fragrance was all locked up in the ice.

The thought came to me, that like the rose we each have the potential to give out the sweet fragrance of God's love to those around us; yet so often we keep it locked inside like a 'frozen asset', until we allow the Lord to melt our hearts and unlock our potential for Him.

2 Corinthians 2 verse 14

"But thanks be to God, who always leads us in triumphal procession in Christ and through us spreads everywhere the fragrance of the knowledge of Him."

A little thanks goes a long way!

As children we were always taught to say 'Thank you' if anyone gave us anything or did something for us.

It's always a good feeling to be 'thanked' because it means that however small the thing we have done, it has been acknowledged; the other person has noticed and appreciated it. We all love to receive praise and it can make a big difference to someone's day if they feel they have done something worthwhile.

God likes thanks too! We are encouraged to thank Him for all His blessings to us, but most important of all to acknowledge the gift of His only Son Jesus.

Appreciating God's love for us by putting our faith and trust in Him, will go a very long way - it will change our life for ever!

Psalm 107 verse 1

"Give thanks to the Lord, for He is good;
His love endures forever."

How are your 'People Skills'?

When applying for Employment these days, one of the questions usually asked is "How are your People Skills"? It's a modern term for "How do you get on with others"?

That's a question we could all do with answering because it applies to our contact with people in our daily lives. I think the real issue is; do we realise how we come across to others? It is a very important question, particularly if we are professing Christians.

Do we perhaps have a proud attitude because we've done well in life and like other people to know it? Maybe we are a bit negative because life has been hard for us and we lack self-confidence? Are we 'known to moan' instead of encouraging others?

However we come across to people, there is always room for improvement. Perhaps we need to ask the Lord to change our thinking and 'hone' our people skills, so folks will be really blessed by knowing us!

Ephesians 4 verse 2

"Be completely humble and gentle; be patient, bearing with one another in love."

Jewels

I imagine that most ladies reading this like jewellery? Probably some have a special item of jewellery that contains a precious stone.

I am fascinated by anything that sparkles, and have watched a jeweller working on a precious stone. When he first takes the raw material in his hand, he looks it over, studies it and thinks about what he will make of it. Then he starts work. Chipping, cutting, filing, heating, polishing. Hours of work, until finally he holds in his hand an exquisite gemstone, faceted and sparkling reflecting the light.

When we come to God with all our shortcomings, He like the Jeweller, starts work on us, and bit by bit , as we allow Him to, He will shape us into someone He can use, who will 'sparkle' for Him.

Will you be like the facets on a diamond, and reflect the light of the Lord to those around you?

Zechariah 9 verse 16

"The Lord their God will save them on that day as the flock of His people. They will sparkle in His land like jewels in a crown."

What's on your mind?

If I asked you the question "What's on your mind"? I wonder what your answer would be. It could be many things are going round in your thoughts. You may have worries and concerns which are disturbing your peace of mind.

Most days our thoughts are occupied with all that we have to do - our families and responsibilities, jobs and so on, but how often do our thoughts turn to God?

He knows every thought before it comes into our mind; He understands and cares about everything that affects us. In the Bible we are encouraged to bring to Him in prayer, all that troubles us and all that we have to be thankful for too.

It always eases a burden if we can talk it through, but even better if the person we share it with can change things for us! Well, God can, so why not 'unburden' to Him today.

Philippians 4 verses 6 -7

*"Do not be anxious about anything,
but in everything, by prayer and petition, with thanksgiving,
present your requests to God."*

Promises

Whilst driving in the city recently, I saw a lorry with a slogan on the side which read "A promise means nothing until it's delivered".

As a little girl from a relatively poor home, I seldom had new things, but one Christmas I was promised a brand new nightdress by a relative. On Christmas morning I excitedly opened the packages I was given looking for my promised gift - but no nightdress! I was bitterly disappointed, and never really trusted their word again.

It's really important in life to be true to our word - even in the little things. Wouldn't it be great if we knew that whatever anyone said to us, they were telling the truth and always kept their promises?!

Thankfully God never breaks His promises. To this very day we are reminded of a promise He made to mankind way back in the days of Noah - we have the rainbow as His seal on that promise!

Genesis 9 verses 12 & 13

I have set my rainbow in the clouds and it will be the sign of the covenant between me and the earth."

Lost your way?

I wonder how many times you have been stopped in the street by someone asking the way because they are lost?

I have had to ask directions myself on occasions and several times I've been sent completely the wrong way, because the person directing me didn't really know the way, but didn't want to admit it! There are times when I've got lost because I missed the signs, got distracted or didn't take time to read the map properly.

We are all on a journey through life, at the end of which there is a destination, but it's here and now that we need to choose which road we take, as only one way leads to Heaven; the Bible is very clear on that. So are you on the right road?

It's no fun being lost, and it certainly won't be at the end of life's journey if we don't end up at the right destination. Putting our faith in Jesus is the only way that will lead us to heaven.

John 14 verse 6

Jesus said: "I am the way and the truth and the life. No one comes to the Father except through me."

A New Song

I've often felt sorry for folks like farmers, milkmen and those who get up very early before it's even light. The only times I have done that have been because I've had to catch a train or plane, or have simply woken up and not been able to go back to sleep!

One morning recently, I woke up before it was light and heard a bird singing. I went quietly and opened my front door to listen. As I did, what I witnessed was amazing!

It was the 'dawn chorus'. I heard bird songs I'd never heard before. The cool spring morning air just rang with the sound, it was all around me and really beautiful. It seemed as though every bird was praising God for a new day and affirming their trust in His provision.

If the creatures raise their song of praise at the beginning of a new day, then how much more should we?!

Psalm 96 verse 1

*"Sing to the Lord a new song,
Sing to the Lord, all the earth."*

Taste and See

I used to have an awful fear of flying and it prevented me from visiting many places I wanted to see. Deep in my heart I knew it was quite irrational, but it was very real.

It's easy to become fearful over things in life, but how can we overcome them? There is a way, but many don't find it easy to do - put your trust in God! You don't need to understand everything about God, or know all about religion, you just have to exercise simple faith. We do it all the time in our daily lives - getting on a bus, paying our money into the Bank, taking pills the Doctor gives us.

One day I read a verse in the Bible where God said I shouldn't be terrified, because He would be with me wherever I went! I asked God to help me overcome my fear of flying - He did and I actually enjoy it now!

Why not take your fears to God - He will give you peace and confidence. You will never know what He can do unless you 'Taste and see'. It could change your life!

Psalm 34 verse 8

*"Taste and see that the Lord is good;
Blessed is the man that takes refuge in Him."*

What's in a Name?

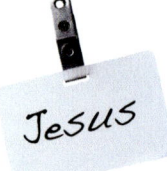

At birth we are each given a name which identifies us. I wonder if you like your name or know why you were given it. However you feel, it is your personal identity and will be so for the rest your life.

Names can have quite an impact on us when we hear them. Some strike fear into our hearts if they belong to evil people. Some warm our hearts as we remember special people by that name. Some even make us smile, especially these days when anything goes!

However, there is one name which is unmistakable as to its owner - Jesus! What does that name mean to you - childhood memories of Sunday School? A name associated with Religious people? or someone very special?

We are told in the Bible that one day the whole world will bow at the name of Jesus!

Romans 14 verse 11

It is written: "As surely as I live" says the Lord,
"every knee will bow before me;
every tongue will confess to God."

'Once upon a time...'

These four words always had a special meaning for me as a child - they usually meant I was sat close to my Grandmother and this was the beginning of a story!

As the tale proceeded all kinds of characters entered into it, lots of things happened; some good, some not, but always at the end, good triumphed over evil and "they all lived happily ever after"!

There is a book which tells a story - in fact it's known as the "greatest story ever told". It starts with four familiar words "In the beginning God…" The difference between the stories read to me as a child and the story in this book, is that this one is fact not fantasy, and it can change our lives.

Best of all, the main character is real, His name is Jesus! He has triumphed over evil and all who read this book and put their faith and trust in Him will certainly "live happily ever after" - in Heaven!

2 Peter 3 verse 13

"But in keeping with His promise we are looking forward to a new heaven and a new earth, the home of righteousness."

About the Author

Cynthia Huddleston (known as 'Ben') was born in Bath and now lives in North Somerset with her Husband Richard.

Brought up in a Christian home, she is the eldest of five children and became a committed Christian at 13 years old.

Her career was as an Executive PA and Office Manager.

She has been involved with a number of Christian organisations over the years including working for Billy Graham on the Mission England Team in Bristol and Christian Television Association (CTA). In 1997 she and her husband went to East Africa as Missionaries with Mission Aviation Fellowship (MAF).

She studied at Capernwray Bible School, Lancashire and has been a Ladies Speaker for over 10 years.